Frogs Can't Flu

By Christel Kleitsch and Joyce Zemke
Illustrated by Tina Holdcroft

D1797835

Jaap Tuinman

CONSULTANTS
Anna Cresswell
Gail Heald-Taylor
Lynda Hodson
Glen Huser

ADVISER
Moira McKenzie

PROGRAMME EDITOR
Kathleen Doyle

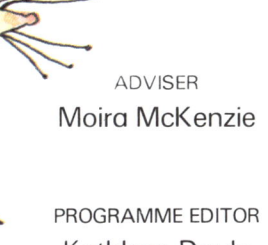

Schofield & Sims Ltd
Educational Publishers

Journeys
Level Four
Frogs Can't Fly

ISBN 0-7217-0552-9

ART DIRECTOR/DESIGNER
Hugh Michaelson

TEACHER CONTRIBUTORS

Terry Bowers
Kaye Hipper
JoAnne O'Gorman
Jan Stevens
Sheila Wittie

Contents

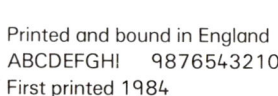

Printed and bound in England
ABCDEFGHI 9876543210
First printed 1984

One Spring Day

One morning Percy Pig looked outside.
"Spring is here!" he thought. "It's time to go out
and do things. I think I'll go and ask Freddy Frog and
Muffles Mole if they want to do something with me."

Percy went to Muffles's house. Freddy
was there, too.

"Let's do things," said Percy. "Let's do
spring things."

"I would like to fly a kite," said Muffles.

"No, no!" said Percy. "I want to go to the lake.
Let's do that."

So they did.

When they got to the lake, Muffles said, "Let's sit here by the lake and tell a story."

"No, no!" said Percy. "I want to find a boat. I want to go out on the lake in a boat."

So they went to find a boat.

They walked and walked and walked.
Then Percy saw a man with some boats.

"How about getting a yellow boat?" asked Freddy.
"I like yellow."

"I would like a blue boat," said Muffles.

"No, no!" said Percy. "I want a red boat."

So they got a red boat.

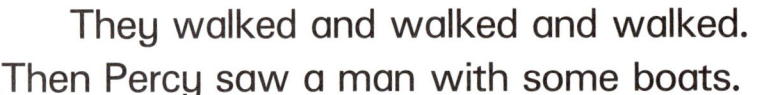

Muffles pulled the boat to the lake.

"No, no!" said Percy. Don't do it like that! This is how you do it."

Percy pulled and pulled. And then PLOP! Percy fell into the lake.

Muffles and Freddy laughed and laughed.

"Some friends you are," said Percy. "I'm all wet and you are laughing at me."

"Some friend you are," said Freddy. "All day you have been telling us what to do."

"Have I?" asked Percy.

"Yes!" said Muffles.

"Yes!" said Freddy.

"OK," said Percy, "I'll stop. But will you do just one last thing that I tell you?"

"Maybe," said Muffles and Freddy.

"Come in the lake with me?" said Percy. "It's fun!"

So they did.

"This **is** fun!" said Freddy.

Muffles Tells a Story

On Fridays they had story time at Mole School. One Friday, Jay Mole said, "Tell us a story, Muffles."

"Yes, please!" said the other moles. They all wanted Muffles because she told a story the best.

"OK," said Muffles, "today I'll tell you a new story."

Once there were three little moles called Stan,
Sally and Max. One day Max looked up and saw
a little white cloud.

"Let's see if we can get that cloud," said Max.
So Max got up on Stan. And Sally got up on Max.

But Sally slid, and down they all fell.
Sally landed on Stan's head.

"Ow!" said Stan.
And Stan landed on Max's head.

"Ow!" said Max.

"We have to think of a new plan," said Sally.

Sally looked around and saw a big stick.
"Look," she said. "If we make a hook
on the end of this stick, we can pull down
the cloud with it."
"Yes," said Max and Stan, "let's try that."

So Max pulled the stick, Stan pulled Max, and Sally pulled Stan.

But the plan was no good. The cloud went by again.

Then the cloud became dark.
"Now I see how to get a cloud!" said Stan.
"We just get some pots — lots and lots of pots."
They put the pots all around.

It rained and rained and rained.

By and by the rain was over. The cloud was gone and there was rain in all the pots.

"That's how to get a cloud!" said Stan.

"And that's the end of the story," said Muffles.

"Thanks, Muffles. That was a good story," said all the moles.

Frogs Can't Fly

"I can fly," said Freddy.

"You? Fly?" said Muffles, and she laughed.

"Oh, Freddy, you are funny," said Percy.
"Frogs can't fly!"

"This frog can!" said Freddy.
"Just come with me. You'll find out."

"Here it is!" said Freddy.

"This thing can't fly," said Percy.
"Where did you get it?" asked Muffles.
"I made it," said Freddy.
"It looks like a bike to me," said Percy.
"It looks like a kite, too," said Muffles.
"How do you fly it?" asked Percy.
"You'll find out," said Freddy.

"Who wants to go for a ride?" asked Freddy.

"Me!" said Muffles.

"Me!" said Percy.

"OK, get on," said Freddy. "Sit over here."

"Oh, boy, this will be fun!" said Muffles.

Freddy rode and rode, but they did not go up.

"Freddy, make it go up!" said Muffles.

"Let's go!" said Percy.

"I can't do it today," said Freddy. "I can't make us fly."

Muffles and Percy got off.

"I said that frogs can't fly," said Percy.

"What a flop!" said Muffles.

Freddy was very sad. He wanted to show his friends that he could fly.

Muffles and Percy started to go home.

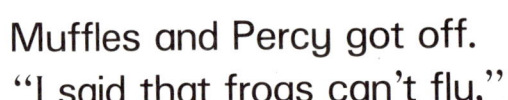

"I'm going to try again," said Freddy. So he got back on.

This time he **did** go up. Up, up, up into the sky.

"One of us can fly on this thing," said Freddy, "but not all three."

"Look up!" yelled Freddy. "Percy! Muffles!
Look up at me!"

Percy and Muffles looked up.

"What's that, way up there?" asked Muffles.

"It looks like Freddy," said Percy,
"but it can't be. Frogs can't fly!"